W9-CLD-169

108

WITHDRAWN

РАЦИОВОЛНА

IRAQ

COUNTRIES IN CRISIS

I.R. BLEAN

Rourke
Publishing LLC
Vero Beach, Florida 32964

© 2008 Rourke Publishing LLC
All rights reserved. No part of this book may be reproduced or utilized in
any form or by any means, electronic or mechanical including photocopying,
recording, or by any information storage and retrieval system without
permission in writing from the publisher.

www.rourkepublishing.com

PHOTO CREDITS: Ceerwan Aziz/Reuters/Corbis: p. 41; Bettmann/Corbis: p. 22; Paul Cowan/istockphoto.com:
p. 42; SPC. Elisha Dawkins/Department of Defense: p. 39; Ali Haider/epa/ Corbis: p. 7; Phan Hatton/Department
of Defense: p. 9; PHC D. W. Holmes/Department of Defense: pp. 28/29; TSGT John L. Houghton JR., /Department
of Defense: p. 6; Hulton-Deutsch Collection/Corbis: p. 19; Ali Jasmin/Reuters/Corbis: p. 34; Klaas Lingbeek-
van Kranen/istockphoto.com: p. 30; Toby Melville/Reuters/Corbis: p. 38; John Moore/Pool/epa/Corbis:
p. 36; Francoise De Mulder/Roger Viollet/Getty Images: p. 27; Chris North/Sylvia Cordaiy Photo Library Ltd:
p. 13; Slahaldeen Rasheed/Reuters/Corbis: p. 5; Ahmed Al-Rubaye/AFP/Getty Images: p. 32; John Said/
istockphoto.com: p. 10; Thaier al Sudani/Reuters/Corbis: p. 4; Mario Tama/Getty Images: pp. 16/17; Time & Life
Pictures/Getty Images: pp. 14, 21; James J. Vooris/USMC/Reuters/Corbis: p. 35; YV/epa/Corbis: pp. 24/25.

Cover picture shows U.S. troops on patrol in Iraq [U.S. Department of Defense].

Produced for Rourke Publishing by Discovery Books
Editors: Geoff Barker, Amy Bauman, Gill Humphrey
Designer: Keith Williams
Photo researcher: Rachel Tisdale

Library of Congress Cataloging-in-Publication Data

Bean, I. R.
   Iraq / I. R. Bean.
      p. cm. -- (Countries in crisis)
   ISBN 978-1-60044-616-0
   1. Iraq--Juvenile literature. I. Title.
   DS70.62.B43 2008
   956.7--dc22

                                    2007020675

Printed in the USA

CONTENTS

CHAPTER ONE

The Battleground

No one knows how many Iraqi people were killed between March 2003, when U.S.-led forces invaded the country, and March 2007. Some say the number of dead is over 60,000, but others have said it could be over 600,000.

We do know, however, that 6,301 Iraqi policemen and soldiers were killed between June 2003 and March 2007. Over the same period, 3,043 Americans, 134 British,

A wailing Iraqi woman kneels before her dead child. He was killed by a bomb left by the roadside, 2006.

Iraqis rush to rescue a passer-by injured by a car bomb. The explosion took place in Kirkuk in July 2006, killing twenty innocent people.

124 military from other nations, and 97 journalists also died.

Every day brought new horrors. In March 2006, 30 bodies were found near the town of Baquba. A bomb killed 85 people in April. June saw 40 innocent people dragged from their cars in Baghdad and shot. In July, 23 people were killed when **terrorists** captured the bus on which they were traveling. Another 53 died when a car bomb went off near a shrine in the town of Kufa. On August 13, 57 people

*November 2003, U.S. soldiers in their tanks in Iraq. The statue in the background was put up by Saddam Hussein, Iraq's **dictator**. The United States hoped that removing Saddam from power would free the Iraqi people.*

recent problems began in mid-2003 when foreign troops, led by the United States, overthrew the country's dictator, Saddam Hussein.

Iraqi politicians then tried to set up a modern, **democratic government**. Many Iraqis supported the idea. Others did not. Some disliked foreign soldiers telling Iraqi people what to do. Supporters of Saddam Hussein led armed rebellions against the invaders.

died when a four-story building was blown up in the capital city, Baghdad. Iraq was in a horrible crisis.

REBELLION

Iraq's crisis is complicated. The country's trouble, as we will see in Chapters 3 and 4, can be traced back to the twentieth century. The

ETHNIC DIVISIONS

This situation grew worse because of Iraq's religious and **ethnic** divisions. In the north, the Kurdish people set up an almost independent state. Meanwhile, the two main **Muslim** groups, Sunni and Shia, fought each other across the rest of the country. They used

The government of Prime Minister Nuri al-Maliki (center), May 2006. After years of dictatorship, the new government was chosen by the Iraqi people in a free election.

bombs, bullets, and knives and targeted anyone who didn't belong to their group. As chaos spread, Iraq came close to collapse.

WE WILL CUT YOUR THROATS

I woke up one morning at 6 A.M. in early April. [In my car], I found an envelope. The note said: 'We will cut your throats within 24 hours. Leave this area, you Sunni pigs.'

Jamal Anour, a Sunni musician who lived in a mixed district of Baghdad

CHAPTER TWO

Cradle of Civilization

Iraq is a country built around two great rivers: the Tigris and the Euphrates. These rivers flow from the north and meet at the city of Basra. They enter the Gulf at one end of the country's 35 miles (56 kilometers) of coast. The rest of Iraq is land locked. To the east is Iran. Turkey is to the north and Syria and Jordan are to the west. In the south, the country borders Saudi Arabia and Kuwait.

WHERE IS IRAQ?

TURKEY

Mosul

Kirkuk

Halabja

Euphrates River

Tigris River

SYRIA

LEBANON

IRAQ is in the Middle East

BAGHDAD

IRAQ

IRAN

Karbala

N
W E
S

JORDAN

An Nasiriyah

Basra

km
0   200
0   200
miles

SAUDI ARABIA

KUWAIT   The Gulf

Kurdish men, from the north of Iraq, wearing traditional dress. This clothing is very different from the long robes worn by Arabs.

People first settled in the region because of the fertile central plain. The area is good for farming. To the north and northeast, the land rises into mountains. Deserts stretch along the southern and western borders. The whole country is hot throughout the summer months.

The winter brings rain, especially to the mountainous areas. Sometimes, there is snow in the north.

DIVIDED LOYALTIES

Iraq has a population of around 26.5 million people. This includes many ethnic groups. Two-thirds of

This 2,800-year-old carving of a winged king was made during the Assyrian period of Mesopotamian history.

the population are Arabs and Arabic is the country's main language. The largest minority are the Kurds who live in the north. They make up about twenty percent of the population.

People have lived in the region for thousands of years. But Iraq as a separate country is very new. People, therefore, often feel more loyalty to their family, tribe, and religion than to their country. This has made uniting Iraq a big problem.

THE FIRST CIVILIZATION

Iraqis are proud that the world's first major civilization developed in their homeland. Over five thousand years ago, the Sumerians of Mesopotamia invented writing and the wheel. They built great cities and learned to irrigate the land beside the Tigris and Euphrates.

After the Sumerian Empire, came the Babylonians and King Hammurabi, when codes of laws were written down for the first time.

The Babylonians were followed by the Assyrians. Their empire fell to the Persians, who were conquered by the Greek army of Alexander the Great in 332 B.C. The Greek and Persian ways of life influenced the region for hundreds of years.

MONGOL INVASION

In 1258, a grandson of the Mongol Genghis Khan was sent to capture Baghdad. The city eventually fell to the Mongols. By then, much of the city was destroyed and possibly up to half a million people, or more, were killed.

FIRST RECORDED LAWS

> If any one steal cattle or sheep, or an ass, or a pig or a goat, if it belong to a god or to the court, the thief shall pay thirty fold; if they belonged to a freed man of the king he shall pay tenfold; if the thief has nothing with which to pay he shall be put to death.

From the law code of Hammurabi, King of Babylon, 1795–1750 B.C.

INVADERS

Mesopotamia changed forever in A.D. 637–638, when Muslim Arabs stormed the land. It became part of a huge Muslim Empire and was ruled by a "caliph," a successor to the Prophet Muhammad, founder of Islam. One of these caliphs, Muhammad's cousin Ali, made Iraq his base. For a long time, it was the richest part of the empire. In 762, the city of Baghdad was founded, and Iraq enjoyed a golden age.

But **civil war**, invasion, and conflict between Sunni and Shia soon ended the period of glory. In 1258, Mongols from Asia flattened Baghdad. They conquered the whole region. Never again would Baghdad be one of the world's great cities.

The famous Spiral Tower of Samarra, built in A.D. 836. It was a minaret. Minarets are the towers from which Muslims are called to prayer.

SUNNI AND SHIA

Islam became divided into two main groups, early in its history. These groups are the Sunni and the Shia. The split came because the two groups could not agree on how new leaders for the religion should be chosen. The Sunni group believe that the first four rulers of the Muslim world are Prophet Muhammad's chosen successors. The Shia believe that only Muhammad's descendants can lead the community.

During the later **Middle Ages**, the region became known as the Two Iraqs. Conquerors from the north and east fought over it.

Stability finally returned in 1534. Suleiman the Magnificent conquered the Two Iraqs and made the region part of his Ottoman Empire.

*Suleiman the Magnificent (1494–1566) was ruler of the **Ottoman Turks** for nearly fifty years. His empire included present-day Iraq.*

CHAPTER THREE

Creation of Iraq

Between 1534 and 1918, the Ottoman Turks ruled Mesopotamia. The territory was divided into three **provinces**: Baghdad, Mosul, and Basra. Without strong government, there was little unity between them. Wars and smaller conflicts were common. Many people returned to a **nomadic** life.

But life began changing in the nineteenth century. Steamboats chugged up and down the rivers. Schools were built, and a postal system was set up, and the country's government improved.

During this time, religious conflicts between the Sunni and Shia Muslims were under control. And the region's large Jewish

Bedouin-people (nomads) have lived in Iraq's desert regions for hundreds of years. They live in tents and travel by camel. Their lifestyle has not changed much over the centuries.

community flourished. Religion was shaping Iraq. The Ottomans favored the Sunni Muslims, who were the minority. Sunnis controlled many important government positions. This gave the group much power. This power lasted long after Ottoman rule had ended.

ENTER THE BRITISH

The British had people in Baghdad as early as 1798. They wanted to protect the trade routes to India. India was Britain's largest and richest **colony**.

During the nineteenth century, the British became more interested in Mesopotamia. Germany did, too.

FLYING IN THE FACE OF HISTORY

" You are flying in the face of four millenniums [four thousand years] of history if you try to draw a line around Iraq and call it a political entity [a country]. You've got to take time to get them integrated. . . .They have no concept of nationhood.

British advisor Gertrude Bell explains why it would be difficult to make Iraq into a country, 1920.

Faisal, the first king of Iraq in 1921. He was born in Arabia. During World War I, he had fought with the British against the Turks.

FAISAL I (1885–1933)

During World War I, Iraq's first king, Prince Faisal I, became known as a diplomat and a warrior. First he tried to create a single Arab state. Then he was king of Syria for a short time before Britain offered him the throne of Iraq. He was accepted by popular vote. As king, he guided Iraq to full independence.

BAGHDAD

Baghdad is Iraq's capital city. It is called the "City of Peace." The city sits between two major rivers and near an important east-west road. Today, Baghdad's population is nearly six million. It is the second largest city in the Arab world. (Cairo is the largest.)

Both countries wanted to expand their influence there. When World War I broke out in 1914, the Ottomans sided with Germany. Britain immediately sent an army from India to Mesopotamia. By 1918, they controlled the whole region.

After the war, the Ottoman Empire was broken up by the British. The three provinces of Baghdad, Mosul, and Basra became a new country: Iraq. Prince Faisal I, one of Britain's Arab **allies** during the war, became its first king. Even then,

Britain had a controlling role in Iraq. Finally, in 1932 the country became independent.

THE REPUBLIC OF IRAQ

By this time, the Arab world was swept up in a wave of **nationalism**. This called for unity between all Arab people. Faisal I's successor was his son Ghazi I. King Ghazi I encouraged this movement. But things changed when Ghazi I was killed in a car crash in 1939. The throne then passed to his three-year-old son, Faisal II. During Faisal II's long

The oil refinery at Kirkuk in 1945. During the twentieth century, Iraq's oil made it one of the richest and most important countries in the Middle East.

Colonel Arif, who had helped get rid of Iraq's king Faisal II, speaks to a huge crowd in 1958. He later took over as the country's president.

BLACK GOLD

The West's early interest in Iraq was due, in part, to the country's oil fields. To keep the fields from enemy hands, the British occupied Iraq during World War II. No one knows how big the country's oil reserves are. Some believe that more than a quarter of the world's oil lies beneath Iraq's soil!

minority rule, his uncle had most of the power. Regard for the monarchy fell.

Anti-British feelings caused Iraq to side with Germany in World War II. In 1941, the British conquered the country again, but their soldiers left once the war was over. Oil wealth was making Iraq an important country. At the same time, there was rivalry between pro-Westerners and Arab nationalists. Eventually, after King Faisal's governments had adopted pro-Western policies, the army seized power. The young king, his uncle, and the first minister were murdered in 1958. Iraq became a **republic**.

CHAPTER FOUR

Saddam Hussein

Iraq had a glorious past and has enough oil wealth for a glorious future. But the country has not reached its potential. This is due to two very difficult questions. First, how could a land divided between Arab and Kurd, and Sunni and Shia, become a united country? Second, what sort of government could bring Iraq stability, security, and fairness without dictatorship?

These problems remained unsolved. Hundreds of thousands of decent people lived in fear and hardship. In Iraq, violence often seemed the only way to make things happen.

On the way up: Saddam Hussein (right), Iraq's vice-president, with General Franco (center), the ruler of Spain. The meeting took place in 1974.

The murder of Faisal II ended the monarchy, but the rule of the new leader, Brigadier Abd al-Karim Quasim was also bloody. In 1963, there was another violent takeover, which brought the **Baath Party** to power. The Baath Party lost power nine months later, but regained power in 1968. A member of the Baath Party, Saddam Hussein, became president ten years later.

SADDAM HUSSEIN'S IRAQ

President Hussein had seen other leaders toppled. He was not going to let that happen to him. This meant removing anyone who might threaten his power. Hussein was soon a dictator. His police force regularly rounded up his rivals. Some rivals were real and some were imaginary. Many people were tortured until they named other suspects, and then they were killed. Thousands of people simply "disappeared." Those left alive were too frightened to talk. Meanwhile, the TV, radio, and newspapers offered nothing but praise for Saddam's government.

Saddam benefited from Iraq's growing wealth. This was due to the high oil prices of the 1970s. The new wealth was not shared equally. Still, most Iraqis felt its benefits. Many could afford cars, air conditioning, and other gadgets for their homes. The health and education services improved.

POWER, WAR, AND DEFEAT

Saddam wanted to make Iraq powerful. One rival was Iran. Luckily for Saddam, the United States government was having trouble with Iran's Shia regime and so decided to back him. Saddam

Iraqi soldiers during the horrifying Iran-Iraq War. Hundreds of thousands of Iraqis died in a conflict that gained nothing.

A parade of soldiers from several nations, 1991. They were all part of the army that drove the Iraqis from Kuwait.

sent Iraqi forces into Iran in 1980, starting the Iran-Iraq War. It lasted eight years. It cost over 500,000 lives—mostly Iraqis—and $800 billion. Both countries were left bleeding and bankrupt.

Only three years later, Saddam took Iraq into another war. In 1990, he invaded tiny, oil-rich Kuwait. The move was condemned worldwide. Early the next year, in the first Gulf War, U.S.-led forces, backed by the **United Nations (UN)**, freed Kuwait. The United Nations hoped that this victory would inspire the Iraqi people to overthrow President Hussein. Encouraged by this, in March 1991 the Shia of the south and the Kurds in the north rebelled

KUWAIT

Britain established Kuwait as a modern state. The country gained independence in 1961. Iraq objected, saying Kuwait had no right to exist because all the land at the head of the Gulf belonged to Iraq. Faced with British troops, however, the Iraqis did not invade. Nevertheless, the Iraqi claim to Kuwait's soil, and the oil beneath it, did not go away. When Saddam Hussein invaded Kuwait in 1990, he was doing what other Iraqi governments had wanted to do!

Liberation Tower, Kuwait. The building honors the forces that freed the country from the Iraqi invaders in 1991.

DOWN WITH AMERICA!

> " America will not be protected from the operations and explosions of the Arab and Muslim mujahidin [religious warriors] and all the honest strugglers in the world. . . .At every available opportunity, we will chase the Americans to every corner. Not even a high tower of steel will protect them against the fire of truth. "

Some of President Saddam Hussein's anti-American remarks during the 1991 Gulf War

against Saddam. Saddam's forces brutally crushed the rebellions. Thousands of people were killed. Over two million Kurds fled into the mountains.

In the 1990s, Saddam Hussein grew more desperate. He defied the United Nations and refused to destroy any **weapons of mass destruction**. The United Nations responded by putting strict **sanctions** on Iraq. This made it difficult for the country to sell much oil. As income fell, poverty and misery rose. The Kurds pressed for independence, and the Shia majority grew restless. From time to time, the United States and Britain launched air attacks on Iraq.

HALABJA

During the Iran-Iraq War, many Kurds in northern Iraq sided with Iran. They hoped to create an independent Kurdistan. During the fighting, on March 18, 1988, Iraqi aircraft dropped poison gas on the Kurdish village of Halabja. Such weapons are banned by international treaty. About five thousand people died immediately. Seven thousand more became ill.

The graveyard at Halabja where five thousand villagers were killed by chemical gas. The forces of President Saddam Hussein used this illegal weapon to crush a rebellion by Iraq's Kurdish people in 1988.

WEAPONS OF MASS DESTRUCTION (WMDs)

For many years, Iraq's neighbors and other countries feared that Saddam Hussein was creating weapons of mass destruction (WMDs). WMDs are weapons that can kill huge numbers of people. The most powerful WMDs are nuclear bombs. Almost more frightening are chemical weapons, including poisonous gases, and biological weapons that spread fatal diseases. At different times during his presidency Saddam tried to develop all these things.

The United States grew angrier with Saddam in 2001. He was almost the only leader not to condemn the terrorist attacks in New York on September 11. Less than three years later, a force of Americans and allies invaded Iraq. Their aim was clear—to remove Saddam Hussein.

CHAPTER FIVE

Regime Change

The United Nations did not support the invasion of Iraq in March 2003. The United States and Britain led the action. They wanted, they said, to destroy Iraq's weapons of mass destruction. The United States also wanted a "regime change." President Hussein's government needed to be replaced by a more democratic government. Whatever the aims, the effects on Iraq were catastrophic.

Iraqi children at school in 2004. Fear of attack and kidnapping had caused many schools to close.

A U.S. tank fires its main gun in the battle for the town of Falluja, 2004. Some experts believed the invasion of Iraq by the United States and others only made the situation within the country worse.

FALLUJA

The Iraqi city of Falluja sits west of Baghdad. It is largely populated by Sunnis, and is known as the "City of Mosques." Falluja was an important center during the Saddam regime. After the allied invasion in 2003, violence in the city erupted. U.S. troops had killed fifteen civilians in a crowd of protestors. U.S. forces recaptured Falluja in 2004. By then, some 25 percent of the city's homes had been destroyed.

The invading forces opened with an air attack. A ground attack from Kuwait followed, and the forces reached Baghdad in less than four weeks. The leading members of Saddam's government were gradually rounded up. The dictator himself was captured that December.

He was tried in an Iraqi court for crimes against humanity and found guilty in November 2006. He was hanged in January 2007.

The invading forces were surprised by two things. First, Iraqi resistance was tough. It continued for months in towns like the Sunni stronghold of Falluja. Losses of life among U.S. forces were expected to be in dozens. Instead they ran into thousands. Second, most ordinary Iraqis did not rush to welcome their "liberators." Certainly

they had not liked Saddam Hussein. But they were suspicious of invaders who appeared to be interfering in

Saddam on trial. Ex-President Saddam Hussein at his trial, 2005. He was found guilty of mass murder and hanged in 2007.

FIGHTING EVIL

> Our most important achievements. . .are two elections and a referendum within a year. Huge numbers of people joined in enthusiastically, ignoring the threats to their lives. . . .The new Iraq, which has recently escaped from tyranny, is bravely building a land where brotherhood, freedom, and democracy will flourish.

Hoshyar Zebari, Iraq's Minister of Foreign Affairs on March 29, 2006

their domestic affairs. Before long, the suspicion turned to resentment.

RECONSTRUCTION

After the war, Iraq needed reconstruction. The broken bridges, shattered power plants, smashed oil-drilling installations, and all the damage inflicted during the fighting had to be repaired. The cost was estimated at $36 billion. Much of the reconstruction work went to U.S. companies. However, the task was much harder than expected. Foreign workers risked kidnap or murder at the hands of Iraqi resistance fighters, known as "**insurgents**."

A provisional government took over governing the country in June

An historic day in 2005. Voters from the south of Iraq stand in line to choose their country's new government. Enemies of democracy attacked some of the voting stations.

2004. A temporary National Assembly (similar to the U.S. House of Representatives) was elected. This body wrote a new **constitution** that the public voted to accept in October 2005. A new National Assembly was elected, and a democratic government was established early in 2006.

CIVIL WAR?

The **coalition's** original plan was to withdraw troops from Iraq once a democratic government was in

Heavily-armed U.S. soldiers look for enemy fighters in the Iraqi town of Dali Abbas, December 2006. Some Iraqis strongly disliked U.S. soldiers being in their country.

place. This proved impossible. By the middle of 2006, violence was tearing the country apart and making life for ordinary Iraqis even more of a nightmare than it had been under Saddam. Kidnap was a daily danger. Bomb attacks made even shopping for necessities a risk. The foreign aid promised in 2003 dried up because no one wanted to invest in such a dangerous country. Schools and hospitals were not rebuilt and skilled workers left the country for employment abroad. The gunmen ruled the streets.

THEY KILLED THEM ALL

> We had a shop, on the main road, for plumbing and sanitation work. They blew it up. This isn't an isolated case. There were many incidents targeting Shia. They killed only Shia—Shia sheikhs [religious leaders] were killed, the Shia grocer was killed, even the baker. They left no Shia people in Amiriya—they targeted and killed them all.

Jasim Adnan, a Shia Iraqi who had lived in the Amiriya district of Baghdad, 2006

What had gone wrong? Perhaps the problem went back to 1920, when the British had created a modern-style country out of three separate provinces? Maybe only a dictatorship like Saddam's could hold together a land of Kurds and Arabs and Shia and Sunni? Once Saddam Hussein was removed, some thought a civil war was bound to happen. Usually, democracy helps people express their wishes and come together. Here it was pulling Iraq apart. If this is true, then Iraq's crisis will end only when the country breaks up. Only time will tell whether this will happen.

Will the killing ever stop? A body is wheeled away after a bomb attack killed dozens of shoppers at a Baghdad market, February 2007.

IRAQI WOMEN

Women were badly treated during Saddam Hussein's regime. Even so, they had more freedoms than women in some strict Muslim countries. For example, they did not have to wear veils. But by 2006, conditions had improved. The new constitution guaranteed women full rights, including the right to vote and to take part in public affairs. To mark the change, the new government included women at the head of four government departments.

*The Iraqi flag flies proud and brave against a clear blue sky.
But what does the future hold for this country?*

TIMELINE

ca.3500 Sumer, thought to be the world's first civilization, develops in Mesopotamia (ancient Iraq). Writing and the wheel are invented.

1792 Hammurabi becomes king of Babylonia.

539 Persians conquer Mesopotamia.

332 Alexander the Great conquers Persia.

A.D.

637 Muslim Arabs conquer Mesopotamia.

762 Baghdad is founded.

1258 Mongols destroy Baghdad.

1534 Ottoman Turks take control of Mesopotamia.

1920 Modern Iraq is created as a British territory.

1921 Faisal I becomes first king of Iraq.

1932 Iraq becomes fully independent.

1958 The military overthrows the monarchy of Faisal II.

1963 Baath Party takeover. Abd al-Salem Arif becomes president.

1979 Saddam Hussein becomes president.

1980 Iran-Iraq War begins. It lasts until 1988.

1988 Chemical weapons are used against Kurdish town of Halabja.

1990 Iraqi forces storm Kuwait.

1991 First Gulf War begins. United Nations sanctions put on Iraq.

1998 Saddam Hussein refuses to cooperate with the United Nations nuclear weapons inspectors.

2003 U.S.-led coalition invades Iraq.

2006 Iraqi Prime Minister Nuri al-Maliki forms a government. Saddam Hussein is found guilty and sentenced to be hanged.

2007 Saddam Hussein is hanged. The fighting and violence continue.

FACT FILE

IRAQ

GEOGRAPHY

Area: 169,235 square miles (438,317 sq km)

Borders: Iran, Turkey, Syria, Jordan, Saudi Arabia, and Kuwait

Terrain: Marshes in the south, desert in the south and east, broad central plain, mountains in the north

Highest point: Unnamed mountain of 11,847 feet (3,611 meters) in the north

Resources: Oil, natural gas, phosphates, sulfur

Major rivers: The Tigris and Euphrates rivers. They meet in the Shatt al-Arab Waterway at the head of the Gulf.

SOCIETY

Population: 26,783,000 **Ethnic groups:** Arab 77%, Kurds 20%, Others 3%

Languages: Arabic, Kurdish, Assyrian, Armenian

Literacy: 40%

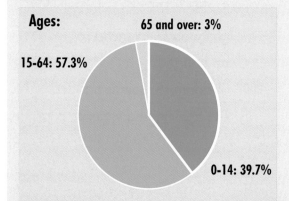

Ages:
- 65 and over: 3%
- 15-64: 57.3%
- 0-14: 39.7%

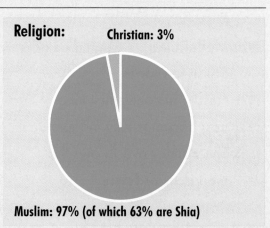

Religion:
- Christian: 3%
- Muslim: 97% (of which 63% are Shia)

GOVERNMENT

Type: Democratic republic   **Capital**: Baghdad   **Regions**: 18

Independence: Fully independent from Britain October 3, 1932

Law: Mixture of European and Islamic set out in the constitution

Vote: All men and women over the age of 18

System: President and 2 deputies (Presidency Council); prime minister and 2 deputies; cabinet chosen by Presidency Council; elected 275-member National Assembly

ECONOMY

Currency: Iraqi dinar

Total value of goods and services (2005 estimate): $94 billion

Labor force (2005 estimate): 7.4 million

Poverty: Unknown of the population below poverty line

Main industries (2005): Oil and oil products, chemicals, textiles, leather, construction materials, food processing, fertilizers

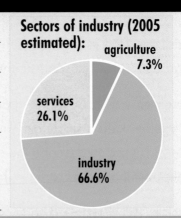

Sectors of industry (2005 estimated):
- agriculture 7.3%
- services 26.1%
- industry 66.6%

COMMUNICATIONS AND MEDIA

Telephones (2004): 1,034,200 fixed line; 574,000 mobile   **Internet users (2005):** 36,000

TV stations: 21 stations, including the state-run Al-Iraqiya

Newspapers: 6 main national papers including Al-Sabah and Al-Zaman

Radio: 80 stations, including Republic of Iraq Radio and Hot FM (Baghdad)

Airports: 110   **Railways:** 1,367 miles (2,200 km)   **Roads:** 28,303 miles (45,550 km)

Ships: 13 over 1,102 tons (1,000 tonnes)   **Ports:** Basra, Khawr az Zubayr, Umm Qasr

MILITARY

Branches: Army, navy, air force—all under reconstruction

Service: All volunteer

GLOSSARY

allies (AL ize) — countries that are sympathetic to each other and will support each other during war

Baath Party (baath PAR tee) — Arab socialist and nationalist political party

civil war (SIV il wor) — war between different groups within the same country

coalition (koh uh LISH uhn) — groups coming together with a single aim or purpose. This term is used to describe the countries that support the U.S. militarily in the war in Iraq.

colony (KOL uh nee) — a country controlled by the government of a distant nation

constitution (kon stuh TOO shuhn) — set of rules by which a country is governed

democratic government (dem uh KRAT ik GUHV urn muhnt) — a form of government where the people elect their leaders

dictator (DIK tay tur) — single ruler not limited by the law

ethnic (ETH nik) — of a racial group

insurgent (in SUR juhnt) — Iraqi rebel fighting the invading coalition of 2003

Middle Ages (MID uhl ajes) — period of history from about A.D. 500 to 1500

Muslim (MUHZ luhm) — follower of the religion of Islam

nationalism (nash uh NAL izuhm) — movement that began in the nineteenth century. It encouraged Arab people to think of themselves as belonging to one nation.

nomadic (NOH mad ik) — wandering from place to place and with no fixed home

Ottoman Turks (OT ur man turk) — Turkish rulers of the Ottoman Empire. At one time the Empire included Turkey and Southeast Europe.

province (PROV uhnss) — region of a country

republic (ri PUHB lik) — country whose government is not led by a monarch

sanctions (SANGK shuhns) — punishments put on a country that has broken international laws

terrorist (TER ur ist) — someone who will do anything, however violent, to achieve his or her aims

United Nations (UN) (yoo NI tid NAY shuhns) — an international organization set up to promote world peace

weapons of mass destruction (WEP uhns ov mass di STRUHK shuhn) — powerful weapons, such as nuclear bombs, capable of killing many

FURTHER INFORMATION

WEBSITES

Aljazeera Magazine

www.aljazeera.com

Arab.net

www.arab.net/iraq

BBC

news.bbc.co.uk/1/hi/world/
middle_east

CIA Factbook

https://www.cia.gov/library/publications/
the-world-factbook

Iraqi Government Website

www.iraqigovernment.org

Website of the Kurdistan Regional Government

www.KRG.org

BOOKS

Ancient Iraq: National Geographic Investigates. Beth Gruber. National Geographic Children's Books, 2007.

Causes of the Iraq War. The Road to War: Causes of Conflict. Jim Gallagher. OTTN Publishing, 2005.

Countries of the World: Iraq. Charles Samuels. National Geographic Children's Books, 2007.

Iraq: Enchantment of the World (Second series). Byron Augustin and Jake Kebena. Scholastic, 2006.

Iraq in the News: Past, Present, And Future. Wim Coleman and Pat Perrin. Myreportlinks.com 2006.

INDEX